BIBLICAL TEXT FROM THE NEW LIVING TRANSLATION

ISBN: 0-8423-7362-4

08   07   06   05   04
6   5   4   3   2   1

Printed in the United States of America

THE PASSION

PHOTOGRAPHY FROM THE MOVIE

THE PASSION OF THE CHRIST

FOREWORD

People often ask me why I wanted to make a film about the Passion of Our Lord. My usual response is that I've wanted to make this film for over ten years, which is true. That seems to answer the question for most.

The reality, of course, is more complex, and had its genesis during a time in which I found myself trapped with feelings of terrible, isolated emptiness. Because I was brought up to be a good Christian and a good Catholic, the only effective resource for me was prayer. I asked God for His help.

It was during this period of meditation and prayer that I first conceived the idea of making a film about The Passion. The idea took root very gradually. I began to look at the work of some of the great artists who had drawn inspiration from the same story. Caravaggio immediately came to mind, as well as Mantegna, Masaccio, Piero della Francesca . . . their paintings were as true to their inspiration as I wanted the film to be of mine. It is one thing to paint one moment of The Passion and be true to it; it is quite another to dramatize the entire mysterious event.

Holy Scripture and accepted visions of The Passion were the only possible texts I could draw from to fashion a dramatic film. But what about the film itself? I wanted the effort to be a testament to the infinite love of Jesus the Christ, which has saved, and continues to save, many the world over.

There is a classical Greek word which best defines what "truth" guided my work, and that of everyone else involved in the project: *alētheia*. It simply means "unforgetting" (derived from *lēthē*—water from Homer's River Lethe caused forgetfulness). It has unfortunately become part of the ritual of our modern secular existence to forget. The film, in this sense, is not meant as a historical documentary nor does it claim to have assembled all the facts. But it does enumerate those described in relevant Holy Scripture. It is not merely representative or merely expressive. I think of it as contemplative in the sense that one is compelled to remember (unforget) in a spiritual way which cannot be articulated, only experienced.

That is the truth I aspired to, as did my friends Philippe Antonello and Ken Duncan, both of whom were often on hand during the filming. Their keen-eyed way of looking and seeing fills this book. The images that move rapidly in the film move more slowly in these photographs, but pull you into the moments they depict. They are, in their own right, pieces of a larger revelation. My new hope is that *The Passion of The Christ* will help many more people recognize the power of His love and let Him help them to save their own lives.

Los Angeles, October 2003

THE PASSION

GETHSEMANE

Then Jesus brought them to an olive grove called Gethsemane, and he said, "Sit here while I go on ahead to pray." He took Peter and Zebedee's two sons, James and John, and he began to be filled with anguish and deep distress. He told them, "My soul is crushed with grief to the point of death. Stay here and watch with me."

He went on a little farther and fell face down on the ground, praying, "My Father! If it is possible, let this cup of suffering be taken away from me. Yet I want your will, not mine." Then he returned to the disciples and found them asleep. He said to Peter, "Couldn't you stay awake and watch with me even one hour? Keep alert and pray. Otherwise temptation will overpower you. For though the spirit is willing enough, the body is weak!"

Again he left them and prayed, "My Father! If this cup cannot be taken away until I drink it, your will be done." He returned to them again and found them sleeping, for they just couldn't keep their eyes open.

So he went back to pray a third time, saying the same things again. Then he came to the disciples and said, "Still sleeping? Still resting? Look, the time has come. I, the Son of Man, am betrayed into the hands of sinners. Up, let's be going. See, my betrayer is here!"

JESUS IS BETRAYED

The leading priests and Pharisees had given Judas a battalion of Roman soldiers and Temple guards to accompany him. Now with blazing torches, lanterns, and weapons, they arrived at the olive grove.

Jesus fully realized all that was going to happen to him. Stepping forward to meet them, he asked, "Whom are you looking for?"

"Jesus of Nazareth," they replied.

"I am he," Jesus said. Judas was standing there with them when Jesus identified himself. And as he said, "I am he," they all fell backward to the ground! Once more he asked them, "Whom are you searching for?"

And again they replied, "Jesus of Nazareth."

"I told you that I am he," Jesus said. "And since I am the one you want, let these others go."

Judas had given them a prearranged signal: "You will know which one to arrest when I go over and give him the kiss of greeting." So Judas came straight to Jesus. "Greetings, Teacher!" he exclaimed and gave him the kiss.

Jesus said, "My friend, go ahead and do what you have come for." Then the others grabbed Jesus and arrested him. One of the men with Jesus pulled out a sword and slashed off an ear of the high priest's servant.

"Put away your sword," Jesus told him. "Those who use the sword will be killed by the sword. Don't you realize that I could ask my Father for thousands of angels to protect us, and he would send them instantly? But if I did, how would the Scriptures be fulfilled that describe what must happen now?" And he touched the place where the man's ear had been and healed him.

Then Jesus spoke to the mob, "Am I some dangerous criminal, that you have come armed with swords and clubs to arrest me? Why didn't you arrest me in the Temple? I was there every day. But this is your moment, the time when the power of darkness reigns." At that point, all the disciples deserted him and fled.

There was a young man following along behind, clothed only in a linen nightshirt. When the mob tried to grab him, they tore off his clothes, but he escaped and ran away naked.

Matthew 26:36-46, 49-54, 56; John 18:3-8; Mark 14:44, 51-52; Luke 22:51-53

My Father! If it is possible, let this cup of suffering be taken away from me.

Matthew 26:39

And they gave him thirty pieces of silver.

Matthew 26:15

See, my betrayer is here!

Mark 14:42

SHLAM RABBANA

Hail, Rabbi.

And Jesus touched the place where the man's ear had been and healed him.

Luke 22:51

They've seized him!

JESUS IS ARRESTED

So the soldiers, their commanding officer, and the Temple guards arrested Jesus and tied him up. First they took him to Annas, the father-in-law of Caiaphas, the high priest that year. Caiaphas was the one who had told the other Jewish leaders, "Better that one should die for all."

Simon Peter followed along behind, as did another of the disciples. That other disciple was acquainted with the high priest, so he was allowed to enter the courtyard with Jesus. Peter stood outside the gate. Then the other disciple spoke to the woman watching at the gate, and she let Peter in.

Inside, the high priest began asking Jesus about his followers and what he had been teaching them. Jesus replied, "What I teach is widely known, because I have preached regularly in the synagogues and the Temple. I have been heard by people everywhere, and I teach nothing in private that I have not said in public. Why are you asking me this question? Ask those who heard me. They know what I said."

One of the Temple guards standing there struck Jesus on the face. "Is that the way to answer the high priest?" he demanded.

Jesus replied, "If I said anything wrong, you must give evidence for it. Should you hit a man for telling the truth?"

Then Annas bound Jesus and sent him to Caiaphas, the high priest.

John 18:12-16, 19-24

Where did he get all his wisdom and the power to perform
such miracles? He's just the carpenter, the son of Mary.
Mark 6:2-3

Inside [the courtyard] the high priest began asking Jesus about his followers
and what he had been teaching them. Jesus replied, What I teach is widely
known. Ask those who heard me. They know what I said.

John 18:19-21

Pilate's wife, Claudia, has a dream.

Matthew 27:19

JESUS BEFORE CAIAPHAS

Then the people who had arrested Jesus led him to the home of Caiaphas, the high priest, where the teachers of religious law and other leaders had gathered. Meanwhile, Peter was following far behind and eventually came to the courtyard of the high priest's house. He went in, sat with the guards, and waited to see what was going to happen to Jesus.

Inside, the leading priests and the entire high council were trying to find witnesses who would lie about Jesus, so they could put him to death. But even though they found many who agreed to give false witness, there was no testimony they could use. Finally, two men were found who declared, "This man said, 'I am able to destroy the Temple of God and rebuild it in three days.'"

Then the high priest stood up and said to Jesus, "Well, aren't you going to answer these charges? What do you have to say for yourself?" But Jesus remained silent. Then the high priest said to him, "I demand in the name of the living God that you tell us whether you are the Messiah, the Son of God."

Jesus replied, "Yes, it is as you say. And in the future you will see me, the Son of Man, sitting at God's right hand in the place of power and coming back on the clouds of heaven."

Then the high priest tore his clothing to show his horror, shouting, "Blasphemy! Why do we need other witnesses? You have all heard his blasphemy. What is your verdict?"

"Guilty!" they shouted. "He must die!"

Then they spit in Jesus' face and hit him with their fists. And some slapped him, saying, "Prophesy to us, you Messiah! Who hit you that time?"

PETER DENIES JESUS

Meanwhile, as Peter was sitting outside in the courtyard, a servant girl came over and said to him, "You were one of those with Jesus the Galilean."

But Peter denied it in front of everyone. "I don't know what you are talking about," he said.

Later, out by the gate, another servant girl noticed him and said to those standing around, "This man was with Jesus of Nazareth."

Again Peter denied it, this time with an oath. "I don't even know the man," he said.

A little later some other bystanders came over to him and said, "You must be one of them; we can tell by your Galilean accent."

Peter said, "I swear by God, I don't know the man." And immediately the rooster crowed. Suddenly, Jesus' words flashed through Peter's mind: "Before the rooster crows, you will deny me three times." And he went away, crying bitterly.

JUDAS HANGS HIMSELF

When Judas, who had betrayed him, realized that Jesus had been condemned to die, he was filled with remorse. So he took the thirty pieces of silver back to the leading priests and other leaders. "I have sinned," he declared, "for I have betrayed an innocent man."

"What do we care?" they retorted. "That's your problem." Then Judas threw the money onto the floor of the Temple and went out and hanged himself. The leading priests picked up the money. "We can't put it in the Temple treasury," they said, "since it's against the law to accept money paid for murder." After some discussion they finally decided to buy the potter's field, and they made it into a cemetery for foreigners. That is why the field is still called the Field of Blood. This fulfilled the prophecy of Jeremiah that says,

"They took the thirty pieces of silver—
the price at which he was valued by the people of Israel—
and purchased the potter's field,
as the Lord directed."

Matthew 26:57-75, 27:3-10

Then the high priest said, I demand in the name of the living God
that you tell us whether you are the Messiah, the Son of God.

Matthew 26:63

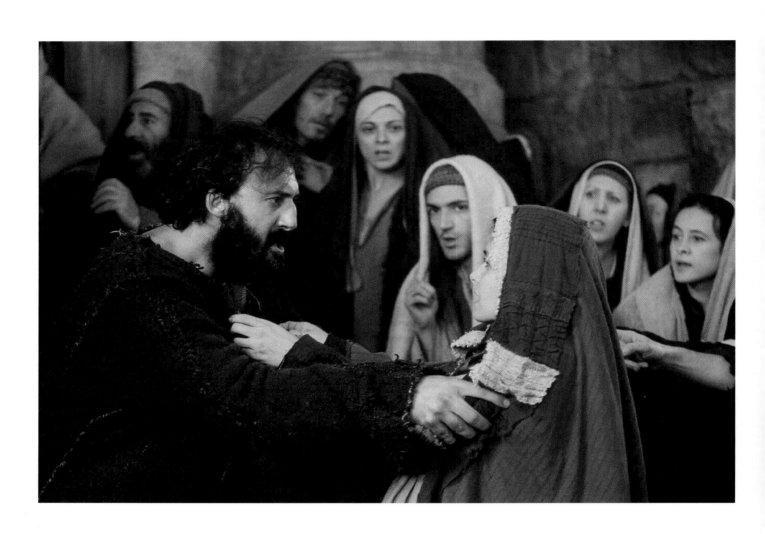

Jesus' words flashed through Peter's mind: Before the rooster crows,
you will deny me three times. And he went away, crying bitterly.

Matthew 26:75

I have betrayed an innocent man.

Matthew 27:4

NOLI HUNC HOMINEM GALILAEUM CONDEMNARE. SANCTUS EST.

Do not condemn this Galilean. He is holy.

JESUS BEFORE PILATE

In the early hours of the morning, Jesus was taken to the headquarters of Pilate, the Roman governor. Jesus' accusers didn't go in themselves because it would defile them, and they wouldn't be allowed to celebrate the Passover feast. So Pilate went out to them and said, "What is your charge against this man?"

They began at once to state their case: "This man has been leading our people to ruin by telling them not to pay their taxes to the Roman government and by claiming he is the Messiah, a king. We wouldn't have handed him over to you if he weren't a criminal!"

"Then take him away and judge him by your own laws," Pilate told them.

"Only the Romans are permitted to execute someone," the Jewish leaders replied.

Then Pilate went back inside and called for Jesus to be brought to him. "Are you the King of the Jews?" he asked him.

Jesus replied, "Is this your own question, or did others tell you about me?"

"Am I a Jew?" Pilate asked. "Your own people and their leading priests brought you here. Why? What have you done?"

Then Jesus answered, "I am not an earthly king. If I were, my followers would have fought when I was arrested by the Jewish leaders. But my Kingdom is not of this world."

Pilate replied, "You are a king then?"

"You say that I am a king, and you are right," Jesus said. "I was born for that purpose. And I came to bring truth to the world. All who love the truth recognize that what I say is true."

"What is truth?" Pilate asked.

Then Pilate went out again to the people and told them, "I find nothing wrong with this man!"

Then they became desperate. "But he is causing riots everywhere he goes, all over Judea, from Galilee to Jerusalem!"

"Oh, is he a Galilean?" Pilate asked. When they answered that he was, Pilate sent him to Herod Antipas, because Galilee was under Herod's jurisdiction, and Herod happened to be in Jerusalem at the time.

JESUS BEFORE HEROD

Herod was delighted at the opportunity to see Jesus, because he had heard about him and had been hoping for a long time to see him perform a miracle. He asked Jesus question after question, but Jesus refused to answer.

Meanwhile, the leading priests and the teachers of religious law stood there shouting their accusations. Now Herod and his soldiers began mocking and ridiculing Jesus. Then they put a royal robe on him and sent him back to Pilate. Herod and Pilate, who had been enemies before, became friends that day.

JESUS RETURNED TO PILATE

Now it was the governor's custom to release one prisoner each year at Passover time—anyone the people requested. One of the prisoners at that time was Barabbas, convicted along with others for murder during an insurrection. The mob began to crowd in toward Pilate, asking him to release a prisoner as usual.

Then Pilate called together the leading priests and other religious leaders, along with the people, and he announced his verdict. "You brought this man to me, accusing him of leading a revolt. I have examined him thoroughly on this point in your presence and find him innocent. Herod came to the same conclusion and sent him back to us. Nothing this man has done calls for the death penalty. So I will have him flogged, but then I will release him."

John 18:29-31, 33-38; Luke 23:2, 4-16; Mark 15:6-8

KAHEL KHAD DI YEHODA' LI NABLATHA DA?

Can any of you explain this madness to me?

REX ES TU?

Are you a king?

My Kingdom is not of this world.

John 18:36

Because Jesus was a Galilean, Pilate sent him to Herod Antipas.
Herod asked Jesus question after question, but Jesus refused to
answer. Then Herod began mocking and ridiculing Jesus.

Luke 23:7, 9, 11

But if I release Barabbas, Pilate asked, what should I
do with Jesus who is called the Messiah?

Matthew 27:22

JESUS IS FLOGGED; BARABBAS IS RELEASED

Then Pilate had Jesus flogged with a lead-tipped whip.

Pilate went outside again and said to the people, "I am going to bring him out to you now, but understand clearly that I find him not guilty." And Pilate said, "Here is the man!"

Meanwhile, the leading priests and other leaders persuaded the crowds to ask for Barabbas to be released and for Jesus to be put to death. So when the governor asked again, "Which of these two do you want me to release to you?" the crowd shouted back their reply: "Barabbas!"

"But if I release Barabbas," Pilate asked them, "what should I do with Jesus who is called the Messiah?"

And they all shouted, "Crucify him!"

"Why?" Pilate demanded. "What crime has he committed?"

But the crowd only roared the louder, "Crucify him!"

"You crucify him," Pilate said. "I find him not guilty."

The Jewish leaders replied, "By our laws he ought to die because he called himself the Son of God."

When Pilate heard this, he was more frightened than ever. He took Jesus back into the headquarters again and asked him, "Where are you from?" But Jesus gave no answer. "You won't talk to me?" Pilate demanded. "Don't you realize that I have the power to release you or to crucify you?"

Then Jesus said, "You would have no power over me at all unless it were given to you from above. So the one who brought me to you has the greater sin."

Then Pilate tried to release him, but the Jewish leaders told him, "If you release this man, you are not a friend of Caesar. Anyone who declares himself a king is a rebel against Caesar."

JESUS SENTENCED TO DEATH

When they said this, Pilate brought Jesus out to them again. Then Pilate sat down on the judgment seat on the platform that is called the Stone Pavement (in Hebrew, Gabbatha). It was now about noon of the day of preparation for the Passover. And Pilate said to the people, "Here is your king!"

"Away with him," they yelled. "Away with him—crucify him!"

"What? Crucify your king?" Pilate asked.

"We have no king but Caesar," the leading priests shouted back.

Pilate saw that he wasn't getting anywhere and that a riot was developing. So he sent for a bowl of water and washed his hands before the crowd, saying, "I am innocent of the blood of this man. The responsibility is yours!"

The crowd shouted louder and louder for Jesus' death, and their voices prevailed. So Pilate sentenced Jesus to die as they demanded. As they had requested, he released Barabbas, the man in prison for insurrection and murder.

Some of the governor's soldiers took Jesus into their headquarters and called out the entire battalion. They stripped him and put a scarlet robe on him. They made a crown of long, sharp thorns and put it on his head, and they placed a stick in his right hand as a scepter. Then they knelt before him in mockery, yelling, "Hail! King of the Jews!" And they spit on him and grabbed the stick and beat him on the head with it. When they were finally tired of mocking him, they took off the robe and put his own clothes on him again. Then they led him away to be crucified.

John 19:1, 4-5, 6b-15; Matthew 27:20-24, 27-31; Luke 23:23-25

*He was led as a lamb to the slaughter. And as a sheep is
silent before the shearers, he did not open his mouth.*

Isaiah 53:7

Before the Passover celebration, Jesus got up and began to wash the disciples' feet. After washing he said, I have given you an example to follow. Do as I have done to you.

John 13:1, 4-5, 12, 15

Many were amazed when they saw him—beaten and bloodied,
so disfigured one would scarcely know he was a person.

Isaiah 52:14

The King of the Jews!

Jesus said to the woman caught in adultery,
Where are your accusers? Go and sin no more.

John 8:10-11

Here is the man! Here is your king!

John 19:5, 14

I am innocent of the blood of this man!

Matthew 27:24

THE CRUCIFIXION

As they led Jesus away, Simon of Cyrene, who was coming in from the country just then, was forced to follow Jesus and carry his cross. Great crowds trailed along behind, including many grief-stricken women. But Jesus turned and said to them, "Daughters of Jerusalem, don't weep for me, but weep for yourselves and for your children. For the days are coming when they will say, 'Fortunate indeed are the women who are childless, the wombs that have not borne a child and the breasts that have never nursed.' People will beg the mountains to fall on them and the hills to bury them."

And they brought Jesus to a place called Golgotha (which means Skull Hill). Two others, both criminals, were led out to be executed with him. All three were crucified there—Jesus on the center cross, and the two criminals on either side.

Jesus said, "Father, forgive these people, because they don't know what they are doing."

The crowd watched, and the leaders laughed and scoffed. "He saved others," they said, "let him save himself if he is really God's Chosen One, the Messiah." The soldiers mocked him, too, by offering him a drink of sour wine. They called out to him, "If you are the King of the Jews, save yourself!" A signboard was nailed to the cross above him with these words: "This is the King of the Jews."

The place where Jesus was crucified was near the city; and the sign was written in Hebrew, Latin, and Greek, so that many people could read it. Then the leading priests said to Pilate, "Change it from 'The King of the Jews' to 'He said, I am King of the Jews.'"

Pilate replied, "What I have written, I have written. It stays exactly as it is."

When the soldiers had crucified Jesus, they divided his clothes among the four of them. They also took his robe, but it was seamless, woven in one piece from the top. So they said, "Let's not tear it but throw dice to see who gets it." This fulfilled the Scripture that says, "They divided my clothes among themselves and threw dice for my robe." So that is what they did.

One of the criminals hanging beside him scoffed, "So you're the Messiah, are you? Prove it by saving yourself—and us, too, while you're at it!"

But the other criminal protested, "Don't you fear God even when you are dying? We deserve to die for our evil deeds, but this man hasn't done anything wrong." Then he said, "Jesus, remember me when you come into your Kingdom."

And Jesus replied, "I assure you, today you will be with me in paradise."

Standing near the cross were Jesus' mother, and his mother's sister, Mary (the wife of Clopas), and Mary Magdalene. When Jesus saw his mother standing there beside the disciple he loved, he said to her, "Woman, he is your son." And he said to this disciple, "She is your mother." And from then on this disciple took her into his home.

Luke 23:26-30, 32-43; Mark 15:22; John 19:20-27

From prison and trial they led him away to his death.

Isaiah 53:8

He was despised and rejected—a man of sorrows, acquainted with bitterest grief.

Isaiah 53:3

BARI

My son.

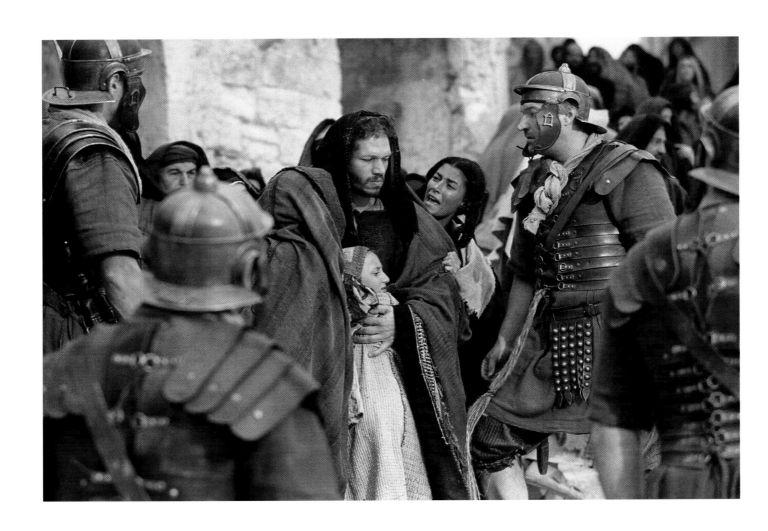

Simon of Cyrene was forced to follow Jesus and carry his cross.

Luke 23:26

They went out to a place called Golgotha (which means Skull Hill).

Matthew 27:33

*I have looked forward to this hour with deep longing, anxious to
eat this Passover meal with you before my suffering begins.*

Luke 22:15

They have pierced my hands and feet.

Psalm 22:16

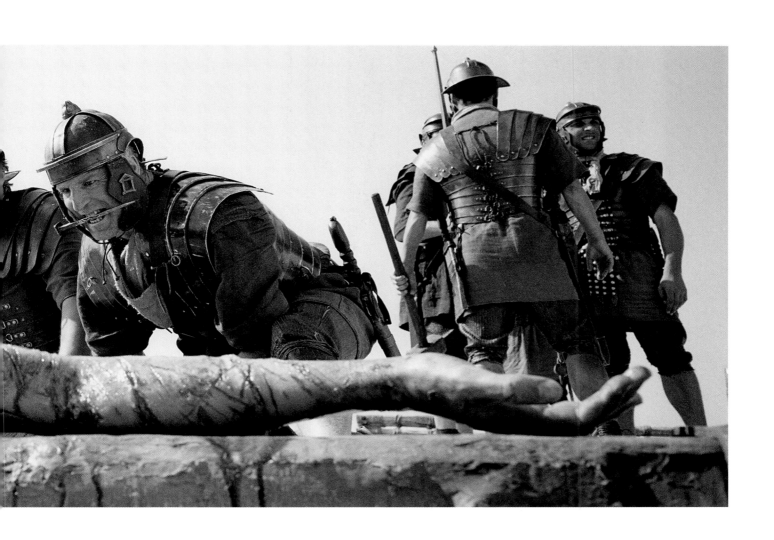

QABBILU LEH AKULU. DNA HU GISHMI.

Take this and eat. This is my body.

from Matthew 26:26

QABBILU SHTEYU. DNA D'MI.

Take and drink. This is my blood.

from Matthew 26:27-28

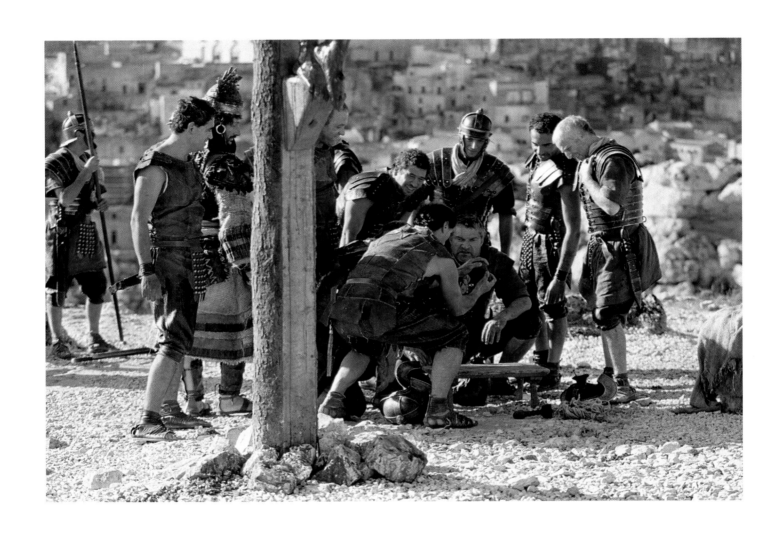

They divide my clothes among themselves
and throw dice for my garments.

Psalm 22:18

I assure you, today you will be with me in paradise.

Luke 23:43

When Jesus saw his mother standing there beside the disciple he loved,
he said to her, Woman, he is your son. And he said to this disciple,
She is your mother.

John 19:26-27

THE DEATH OF JESUS

At noon, darkness fell across the whole land until three o'clock. Then, at that time, Jesus called out with a loud voice, "Eloi, Eloi, lema sabachthani?" which means, "My God, my God, why have you forsaken me?"

Jesus knew that everything was now finished, and to fulfill the Scriptures he said, "I am thirsty." A jar of sour wine was sitting there, so they soaked a sponge in it, put it on a hyssop branch, and held it up to his lips. When Jesus had tasted it, he said, "It is finished!" Then he bowed his head and gave up his spirit.

At that moment the curtain in the Temple was torn in two, from top to bottom. The earth shook, rocks split apart, and tombs opened. The bodies of many godly men and women who had died were raised from the dead after Jesus' resurrection. They left the cemetery, went into the holy city of Jerusalem, and appeared to many people.

The Roman officer and the other soldiers at the crucifixion were terrified by the earthquake and all that had happened. They said, "Truly, this was the Son of God!" And when the crowd that came to see the crucifixion saw all that had happened, they went home in deep sorrow.

Some women were there, watching from a distance, including Mary Magdalene, Mary (the mother of James the younger and of Joseph), and Salome. They had been followers of Jesus and had cared for him while he was in Galilee. They and many other women had come with him to Jerusalem.

The Jewish leaders didn't want the victims hanging there the next day, which was the Sabbath (and a very special Sabbath at that, because it was the Passover), so they asked Pilate to hasten their deaths by ordering that their legs be broken. Then their bodies could be taken down. So the soldiers came and broke the legs of the two men crucified with Jesus. But when they came to Jesus, they saw that he was dead already, so they didn't break his legs. One of the soldiers, however, pierced his side with a spear, and blood and water flowed out. These things happened in fulfillment of the Scriptures that say, "Not one of his bones will be broken," and "They will look on him whom they pierced."

Mark 15:33-34, 40-41; John 19:28-30, 31-34, 36-37; Matthew 27:51-54; Luke 23:48

My God, my God, why have you forsaken me?

Mark 15:34

It is finished!

John 19:30

The curtain in the Temple was torn in two, from top to bottom.
The earth shook, rocks split apart, and tombs opened.

Matthew 27:51-52

JESUS IS BURIED

Afterward Joseph of Arimathea, who had been a secret disciple of Jesus (because he feared the Jewish leaders), asked Pilate for permission to take Jesus' body down. When Pilate gave him permission, he came and took the body away. Nicodemus, the man who had come to Jesus at night, also came, bringing about seventy-five pounds of embalming ointment made from myrrh and aloes. Together they wrapped Jesus' body in a long linen cloth with the spices, as is the Jewish custom of burial. The place of crucifixion was near a garden, where there was a new tomb, never used before. And so, because it was the day of preparation before the Passover and since the tomb was close at hand, they laid Jesus there.

THE RESURRECTION

Early Sunday morning, while it was still dark, Mary Magdalene came to the tomb and found that the stone had been rolled away from the entrance. She ran and found Simon Peter and the other disciple, the one whom Jesus loved. She said, "They have taken the Lord's body out of the tomb, and I don't know where they have put him!"

Peter and the other disciple ran to the tomb to see. The other disciple outran Peter and got there first. He stooped and looked in and saw the linen cloth lying there, but he didn't go in. Then Simon Peter arrived and went inside. He also noticed the linen wrappings lying there, while the cloth that had covered Jesus' head was folded up and lying to the side. Then the other disciple also went in, and he saw and believed—for until then they hadn't realized that the Scriptures said he would rise from the dead.

John 19:38-42, 20:1-9

The one who existed from the beginning is the one we have heard
and seen. We saw him with our own eyes and touched him with
our own hands. He is Jesus Christ, the Word of life.

1 John 1:1

THE FILMING

02/13/04

To My Big SISTER Raquel—

I saw this book & I knew immediately that it was for you. You inspire me more than you could ever possibly know. Your realness & dedication to your relationship with God only makes me want to try harder to atain that same thing I see in you everyday; in myself. I love You very much & I hope this birthday is great for you!

♡ always,

— Your Baby Sis —

Jaci